You would have to go back to bare knuckle days
to find a champion with the pedigree of Tyson Fury, a man born into a family of Irish travelers with boxing in their blood. His proud father Gypsy John Fury was a bare knuckle fighter, his grandfather fought the legendary Len Harvey for a British title. Cousin Andy Lee held the WBO middleweight crown. Another cousin is Hughie Fury, a top heavyweight. Hughie's father, Peter, is Tyson's trainer.

Tyson Fury was named *Ring* magazine's 2015 fighter of the year after his shock defeat of the so-called 'Invincible' Wladimir Klitschko. *Ring* said Tyson "Turned the glamour division upside down."

Mike Tyson, after whom the champion is named, says he is "The best world heavyweight champion since myself."

WBC champion Deontay Wilder is undefeated after 36 fights and called the *Bronze Bomber* for two reasons. One, he won a bronze medal at the 2008 Olympics and two, nobody is claiming he's anywhere near the class of the original *Brown Bomber* Joe Louis. Wilder has a tremendous right hand with over 30 KOs to its credit and is a disciplined fighter, prepared to stick to a plan and wear opponents down before they go.

When Wilder steps into a ring with Fury a good fight is guaranteed. He has the ability to fight in long, sustained attacks and apart from one knockdown in his pro career he can keep his chin out of danger. Tyson Fury is wilder, often more exposed and has been put down a couple times. But he also has the priceless advantage of sheer size, he is two inches taller – and has a two inch reach advantage.

In a mixture of boxing theatrics and showbiz Fury climbed into the ring after a Wilder title defense and sang a soccer style chant, "There's only one Tyson Fury". He also told Wilder he was a 'bum' and he would fight him anytime, anyplace. Wilder responded by telling him he was a 'phoney' and he wasn't playing those games but he would meet him and beat him. The fight will happen, nobody knows when. It all depends on the Fury/Klitschko return. But first let's get back to the ***Rumble on the Rhine*** as it might have been called in a Don King promotion.

The place is Tyson Fury's dressing room in Dusseldorf, Germany. The time is late November and the first heavy frosts of winter have begun to bite on the neat pavements of this prosperous Rhineland capital. What nobody outside the Fury family knows is that the orderly, controlled world of the Klitschko kingdom is about to be blown apart. Yet the myth that nobody around today can beat Vladimir is strong – and with good reason.

In Germany he is loved, respected and hailed as Doctor Steel Hammer. Wladimir Klitschko is the holder of four world heavyweight titles and has seen off all challengers, winning a record 28 title fights - more even than the legendary Joe Louis. His consistent performances have seen opponents stumble, crumble and finally hit the canvas. Many left the ring lesser men than when they climbed in. They were beaten physically and often mentally.

In his mind Wladimir has already dismissed Tyson Fury. Unlike Tyson he is a serious character, a champion schooled by the esteemed Emanuel Seward and winner of 64 fights. Tyson had fought only 25 times as a professional, often against journeymen. At a pre-fight press conference he made a jokey appearance dressed as Batman and capered around the room. Never was the phrase 'fooled by appearances' more appropriate.

Visiting Tyson's dressing room is Wladimir's brother Vitali, an outstanding former heavyweight champion and now a respected politician in the Ukraine. He is there to inspect Fury's hand bandages but Tyson can't resist needling him. He tells him he is going to beat his brother and says "I want you next."

Vitali has heard stuff like this before, inside and outside the ring. His homeland has to face a hostile Russia and confrontation is the name of the game. He smiles as Tyson asks him to sign the bandages with kisses, "I'll do better than that," and inscribes them with love hearts.

Earlier in the day Tyson's trainer, his uncle Peter Fury, had made a discovery that made him threaten to call the fight off. He inspected the ring and when he stepped into it he was horrified. "It was like walking through sticky toffee," he said. The crafty Klitschkos had come up with a plan to counter Tyson's greater speed and mobility. Almost an inch of foam padding had been put under the surface. As a result the deceptively fast Tyson would have been slowed to Wladimir's plodding pace.

At first the Germans refuse to strip the padding out but fortunately a member of Britain's Boxing Board of Control is there. He says "In 40 years I've never seen anything like this. It has to come out." Eventually it does but this incident is one more example of the control the Klitschkos exert in every contest. In professional sport it is often the difference in the margins that makes the difference and so far the champion's team have called the shots in all his title defenses.

Not this time. The Fury camp is determined to start winning *before* Tyson climbs into the ring. Gloves are another big issue. A pair of German gloves sent to Tyson for his approval before the fight are totally unsuitable. "The thumbs are too big, I risk breaking a thumb every time I throw a jab," he says. The reply from the manufacturer comes back that these are the gloves Wladimir uses and he won't use any other. Tyson demands a change – and now the story is that they can't make another pair in time for the contest. We're not having that say father John and trainer Peter - make them! The real issue says Tyson is that Klitschko's preferred gloves are for defensive fighters – and that's not his style. Finally he gets gloves he's happy with. Another win for team Tyson.

Back to fight night and one more opportunity to upset the champion's camp. They make a legitimate protest when they discover that Wladimir has had his hands taped – without supervision from the opposing camp. In any championship contest this is a non-starter although the Klitschkos have probably got away with it in the past.

Once again the Fury camp steps in and demands a change. The Klitschkos are forced to strip the taping off and start again. This time watched by Tyson's advisor Asif Vali. In the vital countdown to the fight Team Tyson had succeeded in putting the Klitschkos firmly on the back foot.

"Tyson is an animal with a cunning, intelligent brain"

Gypsy John Fury, Tyson's father

The drama of Tyson's birth is a well known story but worth repeating because no other father and son history goes quite like this.

When Tyson was born prematurely as a 1lb baby doctors predicted he would always be weak and sickly, his very survival was in doubt. Yet in a moment of supreme confidence his father named him Tyson after the magnificent Mike Tyson who was heavyweight champion at the time.

John then predicted that his son would become world heavyweight champion.

27 years later, speaking in Dusseldorf, he made another prediction. "Tyson's not only here to box but change the world. Wladimir Klitschko can't beat my son."

It had been a turbulent time for John Fury who was released from jail after serving five years of an eleven year sentence for a fight in which he gouged a man's eye out.

Fighting isn't just a pastime for the Fury family, it's a way of life. In his early years John fought bare knuckle bouts and was an unlicensed boxer before turning professional as Gypsy John Fury. He had 13 pro fights, winning 8. Tyson and his brother used to spar with their father from an early age, using tea towels as gloves. As Tyson says, he is the 10th generation of Fury fighters, there are 200 years of tradition behind him every time he steps into the ring. The family has always been around him. His late uncle Hughie Fury, who died tragically early, trained Tyson as he reached British and Commonwealth championships.

The fight that ended with John Fury in jail was part of a feud in the gypsy community and he says he was literally fighting for his life.

Now his son was fighting for the championship of the world and the fortune that goes with it. The Fury family was never in rags but it was about to win serious riches.

Out Thinking The Champion

The campaign that was to end with the defeat of the Klitschkos had started years before. When Paris, his wife to be, was just 16 he told her that one day he would be heavyweight champion. At the time he wasn't much older.

Over the years trainer Peter Fury had studied the Klitschko formula closely. So far it was highly successful but in his view it hadn't moved on to meet changing circumstances. His strategy would take advantage of that.

As Klitschko gets older he needs time and space to get his shots off, he has to set himself. In the gym Tyson worked hard to stop that happening. He was building explosive power to jolt the champion out of his comfort zone and play with his mind.

He fought 12 rounds a day with sparring partners

who were all around the 6' 6" mark. In contrast Klitschko found it hard to find sparring partners close to Tyson's size. When he got into the ring with him it was a real shock.

One of Tyson's sparring partners was a kickboxing champion. Another of the training team taught Tyson to do special jumps that would inject a vital snap into his performance. Everything was designed by Peter Fury with one aim in mind. What will upset Klitschko most? Extra speed and flexibility were essentials. Tyson trained to fight at a high tempo, faster than the champion's usual pace. The focused challenger came into the ring lighter than ever before.

Klitschko is the sort of manufactured fighter who does well when a genius trainer like Emanuel Steward is in charge, watching every move, coaxing a performance out of his man. Above all, adapting his game to what's in front of him. Without Steward he failed to do that.

After Steward died Klitschko didn't replace him with a similar trainer, he went with Johnathon Banks who had been an assistant to Steward and was a regular sparring partner. Banks and Klitschko had worked together for a long time and they get on well but the difference in status of the two trainers is massive. Over his career Steward trained many world champions and was acknowledged as one of the sport's legends. He was in Lennox Lewis's corner when he beat Wladimir's brother Vitali.

Banks still has a career inside the ring and he's also six years younger than Klitschko. Inevitably he lacks the authority and, crucially, the experience of Steward when it comes to plotting the strategy for a title fight.

On the night Klitschko never had the answer to Tyson's boxing skills, his size and his game plan. Tyson's movement was something he couldn't cope with. Both physically and mentally he wasn't at the races.

As usual he was relying on his thunderous jab to soften his opponent up but Fury's footwork stopped that. Tyson threw his jabs and right hands – then skipped away before the champion could throw anything serious in return. Fury is six foot nine but has the agility of a gymnast. He also has a three inch longer reach than Klitschko. On top of that, Tyson is three inches taller than the champion.

The first of those statistics had a devastating effect physically as Tyson's left jab hammered up a big points lead - with not enough coming in return.

The second jarred Klitschko psychologically as he stood face to face in the ring, looking up at a much bigger man.

At the weigh-in and in press conferences he wore platforms in his shoes to minimize the difference.

In the ring he had to confront the reality and he didn't like it, usually he towered over opponents. Size always counts in the mentality of a fighter. The great Sonny Liston was a truly dominating figure, his aura and physical presence usually intimidated opponents long before the fight started. Yet he played tricks to make himself look even bigger. He draped towels across his shoulders underneath his ring robe.

The fight stats tell a lot of the story, Fury landed over 30% more punches than Klitschko, 86 to 52. He caught him with more than twice as many power shots, 48 to 18 and threw almost three times as many hits, 202 to 69.

Right from the off Fury was bombing punches. In the first two rounds he landed 4 power shots to Klitschko's 1. He kept trying to draw Klitschko out but the champion wouldn't take a risk. Tyson's speed made the older man feel vulnerable, he went into his shell and refused to pull the trigger of his powerful right hand, the famous steel hammer. He was always a cautious fighter but now he sensed that if he opened up and tried to throw big punches he was in even more trouble.

Just as importantly, Fury was usually out of reach. The big man's mobility was exceptional, the long, hard training had improved his stamina and the age gap was working for him.
In the seventh Fury even put his hands behind his back, taunting the champion. He landed a jab then a right hand – and did it again as Klitschko tried to counter. He was faster to the punch and outside the ring Wladimir's brother Vitali grimaced in frustration. He could see the fight slipping away, even if the champion didn't .

It wasn't until the 9th that Klitschko finally landed a big right hand that shook Fury. He show boated in a 'is that the best you've got' kind of way and came back with a solid left that had the champion scrambling. In the 11th Fury was deducted a point for rabbit punching but it was a rare loss of control.

From the 9th onwards Klitschko's corner had been telling him he had to knock Fury out to hold onto his title but it was wasn't until the 12th that he cut loose and started swinging. He connected a couple of times but Fury was still in charge and the decision was unanimous, a clear points win that not even the champion's camp tried to dispute. His fans in the stadium were puzzled as well as disappointed. The real Wladimir just hadn't showed up.

In the US the TV audience definitely had. Even though the fight wasn't on in prime time there were over a million viewers. TV executives were impressed and started discussions about the likely re-match. After a long period of over-dominance by the Klitschko brothers the heavyweight division had a new champion with speed, strength, charisma and talent, a man who could communicate with fans and sell tickets. He was outspoken and controversial, different in many ways but reassuringly familiar in one. His Irish background was set to win him support across the continents.

After the fight Tyson was generous in his praise of Wladimir calling him a great champion and hoped he would be as good. He apologized for his rowdy pre-fight behavior putting it down to enthusiasm but he also said the heavyweight division would now be about entertainment as well as honor and glory. To prove the point he burst into song when he saw his wife. He sang the Aerosmith hit 'I don't want to miss a thing' as Klitschko looked on.

The ex-champion looked like he wanted to be missing and away that very second. But as former heavyweight champion David Haye said, the end of the Klitschko reign is good for boxing. "As long as the titles stayed in Germany nobody cared." Haye is no friend of Tyson and the feeling is mutual. The new champion said Haye was a coward and he would never give him a title shot.

That's for the future and Haye has to earn the right to a shot anyway but grudge matches are always good box office. First there was a lot of talking to be done and Tyson has never come up short in that department. Talk, headlines and tension have been huge forces in boxing ever since promoter Tex Rickard first created an explosive mix of controversy, chaos and media fireworks to launch the modern game with showbiz glitz.

That was in the roaring twenties during the bruising days of Jack Dempsey. He was a champion who made it all the way to Hollywood, combining brutality in the ring with style on the screen and it paid off handsomely.

After the night in Dusseldorf the spirit of Rickard was back. The dozy days of the Klitschko reign were over although talk of the re-match started immediately.

Financially successful fighters create their own headlines, boxing fortunes are built on them. But Tyson got off to a bad start with the wrong kind of headlines as he appeared to link homosexuality with pedophilia. His trainer Peter Fury gave a different view, saying on a BBC Radio Five Live show that he had spoken at great length with him. He said 'Homosexuality is two consenting people. Pedophilia isn't so there's a vast difference.
One is an evil act and the other is between two consenting people. It would be a dangerous message if that's how it came across. Tyson is happy to give a public apology and explain in detail exactly what he means. It's not a problem at all. It was taken out of context.'

Possibly the biggest obstacle to understanding where Tyson is coming from is that he has been born and brought up in a different world to any form of conventional, nine to five life. As he says himself, "People should understand that our lifestyle is totally different. We may be the same colour and we may speak the same language but deep inside we are nothing alike. We are aliens."

As Tyson describes it the travelling community lives in a muscular, macho world where men rule in all matters and family ties are everything. As a world heavyweight champion he will find that his world is going to collide, sometimes violently, with accepted ideas about how life is lived in the 21st century. To complicate the arguments further he is a born again Christian who gave God the credit for his victory over Klitschko and he takes strong religious values into every area of his life.

Totally rejecting claims that he hates homosexuals he told journalists, "All I can say is we don't hate anybody. Jesus loves the world, as do I."
Tyson's public world is in the boxing arena and it should never be forgotten that this is an extreme sport. Getting punched for a living, dedicating your life to it, making daily sacrifices for the sake of training is not a choice many can even think about.

Angelo Dundee trained Muhammad Ali and was at the heart of the sport for 50 years. He spoke from the inside when he said, "Boxing's a tough hustle. It takes a special kind of guy to be a fighter."

It shouldn't be surprising that a man who may well turn out to be Britain's most outstanding heavyweight fighter is not someone who slots easily into the accepted public role of a professional sportsman. A Gary Lineker or David Beckham for example.

He is different, from the outside of conventional society and if he comes 'inside' it will be on his terms. He points out that he beat a man nobody else was beating. One who many said couldn't be beaten. He did so convincingly just as he has been happy to do in the past when he has had "hundreds of challenges" at Traveler gatherings.

Many fancied their chance and he took them on, enjoyed beating them and carried on with his life. Even as heavyweight champion he'd be happy to do the same again, he has the confidence of a fighter and a sense of his own destiny. As his father John said after the Klitschko fight, "You should listen to us, we'll not be talked down to."

Heavyweight Champion Makes First Media Appearance – in Bolton!

It was yet another shock to the boxing world. The new champion's first media appearance in the UK wasn't in London's West End or even Wembley stadium. TV camera crews and the press had to travel north to the ground of Bolton Wanderers Football Club, the Makron stadium.

Alongside a retail park, with a fine view of Rivington Pike in the West Pennines, this isn't home counties country, far from it. But it is close to Tyson's birthplace in Manchester and Bolton is home to his advisor Asif Vali. This was a sign to the media that the new champion is not a creation of the gilded south east and in future he will be calling the shots.

If Bolton is known as tripe and trotter country, the venue for Tyson's second fight after he turned professional was just as down to earth in nearby Wigan, famous as the land of the pie eaters.

He was twenty and beginning a series of what his promoter Mick Hennessy described as learner fights. The man in the other corner was Marcel Zeller, a thirty six year old campaigner with a string of twenty knock out wins on his record and three defeats. Zeller can punch, he doesn't rely defense and back himself to land a big one. Before the fight he told Tyson, "I'll either knock you out or lose."

When the bell went Zeller came out body punching and this looked to be the only part of Tyson he was likely to hit. The younger man towered over him, had a much longer reach and a two stone weight advantage. In round one Tyson backed him into a corner with combination head and body punches as Zeller crouched behind his gloves. He made the mistake of motioning Tyson in. He obliged with a right hand that visibly rocked Zeller.

For a moment it looked like it was going to be a very short learning experience but Zeller survived to the third round before the referee wisely stopped it. Zeller couldn't get out of the corner or throw punches because Tyson was ripping off uppercuts and not even breathing hard. Afterwards he confessed he had only just started eating the right foods and training properly. He asked boxing supporters to imagine how he would look further down the line when he was fighting fit – and had a stronger boxing education. Fury brought a big fan club to Wigan. Early on in his career he was proving he could pull the crowds and stop journeymen fighters in their tracks. Could he go further?

Team Tyson had no doubts at all and the word was spreading. Here was the talent British fans had been praying for, year after year without success. The world heavyweight division had fresh hope on the horizon - as Mike Tyson himself was to recognize later.

More Wins - Then A Bump In The Road

Tyson continued in the professional ranks winning and learning as he went. In seven months after the Zeller fight he stopped five opponents inside the distance. But when he met John McDermott he needed a huge slice of luck. McDermott is no classical fighter, his favorite tactic is to throw big roundhouse rights, keep coming forward and look to knock his man out.

He made Fury look the young, inexperienced and raw fighter he was at this stage. Fury couldn't cope with McDermott's durability and constant pressure. The problem for McDermott was that referee Terry O'Connor had one of those nights where the fans were screaming highway robbery. O'Connor scored Fury six points clear in a ten round fight which was probably a travesty of what actually happened. He missed McDermott's steady piling up of points in favor of Tyson's flashier, shorter bursts of punching. Cynics would argue that Tyson got the verdict because he was the more marketable fighter. Even bigger cynics might say that when O'Connor lifted Fury's arm he was thinking back to a night years earlier when McDermott's father had hammered his own father. As for McDermott's promoter Frank Maloney – he had a heart attack after the decision. It was that kind of night.

There had to be a re-match and this time Tyson looked the sharper, more determined fighter. He showed real speed with his right hand punching and also looked to have more stamina. With McDermott tiring Tyson landed a left and right that put him on the floor late in the eighth round. The older man looked exhausted and the extreme heat in the hall wasn't helping him.

Even so McDermott was up quickly, just before the bell and came out for the ninth determined to fight back. Yet it was Tyson who was the stronger and he put McDermott down twice. The referee stopped it and Tyson had deservedly won a revenge match. His youth, strength and speed had taken him through and this time there were fewer arguments.

After this the talk was of a fight with Dereyk Chisora for the British heavyweight title but it was premature. Tyson needed more fights to extend his experience and develop his technique. So far his sheer size and strength had let him get away with wild swinging that would leave him open to a quality counter puncher.

The next man up was American heavyweight Rich Power who came to the York Hall in Bethnal Green with an unbeaten 12 fight record including nine knock outs. He took the fight at just one week's notice and deserved every credit for putting his unbeaten status at risk. It was a risk too far.

Tyson towered over him, had a clear reach advantage and was three stones heavier. The big man went for a quick knock out with some fast right hands but Power bravely stood his ground and took the punishment. He was put down by a body shot but got up and went the distance. Tyson won every round and his performance against a man rated 18th in the world didn't go unnoticed in the US. His talents and style were winning important friends. The fight marked another stage, it was a useful part of the Fury learning curve.

Emanuel Steward Looks Into The Future

Manny Steward trained 41 world champions including Thomas Hearns, Lennox Lewis and Wladimir Klitschko. Together with Angelo Dundee he was one of the greats.
He was working with Klitschko around the time when he first got a good look at what Fury could do. Speaking years later, Tyson said that Klitschko was there when Manny delivered his verdict and said, in his opinion, Tyson was a future world champion. There is no record of how Klitschko took this news of a strong rival. But it may be the reason why he was so hesitant the night he met Fury. Like many insiders in the fight business he had tremendous respect for Manny and his judgement.

Manny had heard about Tyson from Andy Lee, Tyson's cousin who he was training and who went on to become WBA middleweight champion. New talent was always welcome at Steward's famous Kronk gym and Tyson was invited to a training camp. He went on to stay with Steward at his home. The great man liked what he saw. He praised Tyson's fast hands, natural boxing talent - and charisma – going so far as to say he was the next Muhammad Ali.

Importantly he also praised his mental strength. At the time he was training two highly rated upcoming fighters, David Price and the undefeated Robert Helenius but in comparing them with Tyson he wasn't sure they had the mental strength to be champions. He felt Tyson was tougher and five years later he would be proved right again.
 Another top US boxing expert Teddy Atlas was just as confident about Tyson, saying during an ESPN streaming broadcast "If Klitschko ever steps into a ring with Tyson Fury he's going to be in serious trouble. He's never met anyone with his combination of size, movement and skill."

Steward didn't live to see his prediction come true but he was with Tyson when he went to Canada to take on the journeyman fighter Zach Page.
Tyson won every round but in between rounds Manny told him he was slipping into a comfort zone, doing the same thing all the time, left jabs and a right cross. Manny said he was predictable, he should mix it up with uppercuts and try to hook off the jab.

In later fights Tyson demonstrated he had the skills to develop as an all round fighter. He underlined his growing ring craft by boxing southpaw – against dangerous opponents.

But Manny also added a word of warning. He told Tyson he was carrying too much weight and needed to stick with a serious training programme.

Carrying The Weight - Packing The Punch

It would be some time before Tyson got around to seriously confronting his weight issues but in the meantime he showed he had the power to take out good fighters.

Brazilian Marcelo Luiz Nascimento was his next opponent and he was no journeyman fall guy. He came into the ring as Latino Heavyweight Champion with a thirteen fight unbeaten record. He had won the title in his last fight with a thunderous left hook in the first round, a TKO against the tough Argentine fighter Gonzalo Basile.

Tyson showed he meant to dictate right from the off. In the first round he shook his man up with straight right hand shots then put him down with a right hook. Nascimento got up but he looked shaken and felt the full weight of Tyson's eighteen and half stone. Ringside fans were expecting Tyson to finish it quickly but Nascimento went into defensive mode with both gloves held high and didn't get many shots off. As the fight progressed Tyson gradually broke him down with fast, sharp body punches and in the fifth he caught him with a right hand that wobbled him. Another one right through his guard did real damage and Nascimento fell face down, landing like a Brazilian tree trunk with arms outstretched. His corner climbed into the ring immediately and it was all over.

After the fight Tyson got into all kinds of controversies by bad mouthing other British heavyweights including the champion Chisora who he called Dereck 'No Good' Chisora.

Chisora responded by saying amongst other things that Fury was 'all boots and braces but no substance'. Fury's problem with Chisora was that he wanted to fight him for his title sooner rather than later but Chisora had a date with Wladimir Klitschko first. Chisora told him to 'wait for his chance like a man' and said he was a 'fool with a horse and a total plonker'.
The insults were flying and critics joined in, usually backing Chisora. One said Fury was 'overweight, overhyped and totally overrated' but fate stepped in when Chisora's proposed shot at Wladimir Klitschko fell through and Fury got his shot at Chisora's British title.
Tyson disappeared into a training camp, determined to get into the kind of shape Manny Steward said he should be. He came into the ring a stone lighter than when he had beaten McDermott and he needed the conditioning because for long periods he was forced to fight Chisora's fight, a slugfest with both men throwing overhand shots

then exchanging punishing body blows. The second round was Chisora's best. He caught Fury with a wide swinging left hand, forcing him to back up and cover up. But tellingly Fury came back strongly and put Chisora on the retreat.

As the fight went on Fury was able to dominate with his left jab and follow up with thumping rights. Chisora's corner told him he had to hit over Fury's jab but he couldn't do it often enough and he resorted to putting his gloves up and taking Fury's jab, taunting the challenger, saying he wasn't hurting him at all. Maybe not but he was scoring points and Chisora was falling well behind.

He wasn't throwing enough punches and midfight his corner even warned him they would pull him out unless he attacked more. Chisora rallied and took the fight to Fury but the bigger man kept him away with his long, accurate jab. Fury's training was paying off. He was younger too and he finished stronger. Even after Chisora staged a desperate last round attack - Fury countered with a barrage of jabs and right hands. A unanimous decision gave it to Tyson and there was a new British champion.

Afterwards he said there had been a lot of trash talking but he had every respect for Chisora and thanked him for giving him the title shot.

Some of the media reaction was grudging. Tyson had a following but it wasn't reflected in press coverage. Some critics just couldn't see what was there, a genuine British prospect who had the ability to storm world ratings. Yet there was more to the criticism than boxing, Tyson was outspoken and many resented him as a brash outsider. Others went further, there was more than a hint of racial prejudice against an Irish traveler.

If critics wanted more humility they were knocking on the wrong door. His life and background as a member of the travelling community had shaped the man. He was fiercely independent, no conformist and aware of how his community was often seen domestically.
Fury was smart enough to know he could turn that to his advantage and appeal to a wider, global audience. He would be the proud Gypsy Warrior and the only way he was going was up.

First he needed more ring education and just two months later he was back in business. His opponent was Nicolai Firtha a top American fighter who came into the ring with the WBA USA heavyweight title. He was 'only' three inches shorter than Fury and had twenty wins with eight knockouts. The fight in Belfast was practically a home town affair for Fury who has a big Irish following. Tyson charged out from the bell and it looked as if he wanted to finish it in the first but Firtha was experienced and capable, he fought back well. But the third round was entirely different and possibly Tyson's most dangerous round as a professional so far. He was getting careless with his left hand held too low. Firtha caught him with an overhand right that smashed into his temple and shook him. He was forced to grab and hold, in real trouble. Firtha landed a couple more and though they didn't have the same power Fury was still retreating at the end of the round.

In interviews after the fight he admitted he was shaken and put it down to experience. He needed to defend better and as even Joe Louis occasionally found, it's dangerous to drop your left hand against a heavy hitter.

Fury had been happy to go into a brawling match with Firtha until the nightmare third brought him back to reality. He went back to fighting behind his jab and controlled the fourth better but still it was an exciting fight for the fans with both men going for it.

Then in 19 seconds of the fifth Tyson landed the punch of the fight. It wasn't a swing or a cross, it was a short right counter – and it caught Firtha smack on the jaw – as he was coming forward. His momentum added to the power and although he didn't go down he was wobbling. Tyson continued to land and the referee rightly stopped it, Firtha was only seconds away from serious damage.

Another Title - But Another Knockdown!

Tyson's fight with Neven Pajkic for the British Commonwealth title was controversial before it started. Tyson called Pajkic out from the ringside in Ontario after the Canadian champion had taken eight tedious rounds to beat the 47yr old German Andreas Sidon.

Tyson said he was the British champion and he'd show Pajkic the difference between a real champion and a joke. Not surprisingly there were angry words between the pair, ending with Tyson saying their fight wouldn't last long and Pajkic would feel the full force of Tyson Fury. Pajkic had made some remarks about Tyson's Gypsy background so everything was set for a wild night, there was Menace in Manchester.

Pajkic came out with his head down, throwing overhand rights. He was hustling and pushing, staying on the inside. His plan was to back Tyson up, stop him landing the jab and dictating the fight.

In the second Pajkic had success as Tyson repeated the mistake he made against Firtha. He dropped his left hand and Pajkic scored with one of his overhand rights. The punch caught Fury full on the jaw with 16 stones behind it. He went straight down, the Canadian champion had dumped him on his backside and Fury's words were coming back to bite him. Pajkic was hugely encouraged and went after Tyson who was holding on towards the end of the round.

In the third the fight swung completely the other way. Tyson caught him with short. clubbing rights to the side of his head as he bored in and Pajkic was hurt. He went down but stood up for the count with the referee looking closely at him before continuing the fight. Tyson went after him and Pajkic literally staggered round the ring before he went down again.

He took a standing count but was determined to continue. He put his gloves up and the referee let him carry on though he knew the end was near. Now Tyson was hitting him at will, nothing was coming back and the referee jumped in to stop it with the fired up Fury wanting more.
Tyson predicted the fight wouldn't last long and it didn't but being knocked off his feet wasn't part of the plan. He was getting an education the hard way, fighting recklessly and a better class fighter than

Pajkic would have made him pay. Yet it was entertaining for the fans and the Manchester crowd was left screaming for more.

Even though promoter Mick Hennessy was handling box office gold he knew it was vital to take Tyson along at the right pace. The risks were as big as the potential, a defeat might shatter Tyson. Even though he seemed to be bursting with confidence he hadn't been tested by defeat yet.

He was still only 23 with just 17 professional fights to his name. Time was on the side of Team Tyson.

Picking Up Two More Titles

When Martin Rogan fought Tyson Fury for the vacant Irish Heavyweight Championship he was giving away 17 years, 6 inches in height and over a stone in weight. It was a big ask although Rogan had a record of 14 wins with 6 knockouts. He started strongly and won the first two rounds. Fury felt confident enough to try a southpaw style saying he was ambidextrous and could knock a man out with either hand.

It was a left hook that began the end for Rogan as he went down in the third. He got up quickly but Fury stood in the centre of the ring and dominated the fight with his jabs. In the fifth Fury hit him with a crashing body shot that left him gasping for breath on the floor. He beat the count but his corner stopped the fight and Tyson was the new Irish Champion. Afterwards there were long celebrations in Belfast with his growing Irish fan base as he took another step along the road to Klitschko.

Tyson travelled to the West Country in England for his next contest, a fight for the vacant WBO Intercontinental championship. He was taking on a battle hardened veteran with 35 wins on his record, a man who had been in with quality fighters like Evander Holyfield.

Vinny Maddalone fought out of New York and had a solid right hand that was his best chance against a bigger man.

Unluckily for him he met a Tyson Fury who was on top of his game. He came out looking busy, throwing his jab and waiting for the chance to throw his own right hand. That came in the first round and Maddalone was surprised by the force. That wasn't his only problem, Tyson was using his footwork as well as his jab, he scored with fast jabs then slipped out of trouble as Maddalone tried to rush him and pin his man on the ropes. The tactic never looked like working as Tyson dominated, using his strength and speed. His right hand was doing real damage and Maddalone's face was an angry red mass, he was taking heavyweight punishment and looked out of his class.

Tyson hit him with jab after jab and he couldn't land a return shot as the Gypsy Warrior showed he had mobility as well as size and strength.

By the fifth Maddalone was battered, cut and bleeding with Tyson landing constantly. After a minute he motioned to the referee to come in and stop the fight, the traffic was so one way. Thirty five seconds later the referee did just that and it was another hugely impressive win.

Tyson was climbing the ladder and learning all the time though now he was ready for a WBC heavyweight eliminator. This was against Kevin Johnson, a man who was unbeaten until he lost to Vitali Klitschko in a world title fight. Johnson took Klitschko the distance and said afterwards he had a muscle injury in the fight, lost his jab and could do no more than defend. In the last round he was taunting Klitschko, saying he couldn't hit him on the chin. Klitschko did just that, landing with a good shot that shook him – but he stayed upright.

Now it was three years later. Johnson had scored another six wins with one defeat and still never been knocked off his feet.

Tyson couldn't stop him either though the result was never in doubt. He outboxed and out jabbed his man and said afterwards he never set out to KO an elusive fighter who was hard to hit and had a good chin. Whether he could have done or not is open to question but up and coming star Antony Joshua became the first man to stop Johnson with a second round TKO. By then Johnson was on a losing streak so comparisons are difficult but Joshua, a Gold medal Winner at the 2012 Olympics, had put down a marker and looked certain to fight Fury at some stage.

Fairytale Of New York

As a student of boxing history Tyson knows about great fighters like Joe Louis, Sugar Ray Robinson and the Irish American light heavyweight champion Billy Conn who gave Joe Louis such a hard time. They all appeared in legendary fights at Madison Square Garden and he was inspired by the idea of making his American debut there, another of his dreams realized.

But this Fairytale journey was to include a severe bump in the road. Boxing teaches us that triumph and disaster are never more than a split second apart and Tyson's opponent Steve Cunningham thumped the lesson home in the second round.

Until then Fury had been showboating, mocking Cunningham, even pushing him contemptuously after the bell at the end of the first.

Then the former two time cruiser weight champion caught Fury with a whipped, overhand right that landed smack on the jaw and dumped him on the floor. Afterwards Tyson said, "I got caught. When you don't see them coming you go down. But you get back up."

Moments like that give promoters of marketable fighters a nasty shock. Tyson was more surprised than shocked and when he got up he was all business. He went back to boxing, fighting behind his fast, heavy jab.

Physically he was on a different plane to Cunningham, 44 lbs heavier and 6 inches taller. He began to make his natural advantages count and rounds three to six were good to watch, especially in the Tyson camp. Cunningham did himself justice, fighting back well and landing a good right hand that made Tyson grab and hold. His problem was that of a good smaller man against a good, much bigger man.

Tyson was leaning on him, wearing him down as he tried to cope with the sheer size of his opponent. Cunningham said it made him feel like he was "fighting two men" and Fury did what "big men do to smaller men".

In the seventh Tyson began what was looking inevitable. He caught Cunningham with a short right uppercut that shook him, setting him up for the brutal end. Tyson used his left forearm to hold him in position on the ropes then delivered the finisher. A right uppercut that smashed straight onto the jaw and put Cunningham down. He was stretched out twitching while Tyson was in the middle of the ring dancing, he knew it was all over. The forearm was street instinct and illegal but Cunningham didn't bother to protest, he had been beaten by the better man on the night.

Tyson acknowledged his opponent, saying he had put up a good fight, worthy of a champion. Then he was off to celebrate, not even stopping for a shower. Together with his wife Paris, his uncle and trainer Peter Fury, plus an entourage of happy fans he moved from bar to bar, drinking Guinness and anything else that caught his fancy. Bystanders wondered what was going on, Tyson was almost unknown in the US and the sight of a bare-chested giant draped in an Irish flag didn't announce that a new force in heavyweight boxing had arrived. The Tyson camp didn't worry about that, they knew what had happened. Their man was on the map in the US.

Yet there was one important area they needed to address. Between his previous fight with Kevin Johnson and his next one with Joey Abell, Tyson put on 26lbs. That was unacceptable and it brought back memories of Emanuel Steward's warning, "He needs to stick to a serious training routine." To give himself a decent chance against Klitschko he had to put in the work and get down to his best fighting weight.

Before he got in the ring with Abell he had made a start by dropping 20lbs since the Cunningham fight. That was 10 months ago and he looked a little rusty. Abell stands a good six foot five and he's a dangerous fighter, a man with thirty Kos in thirty seven fights. In the first round he showed his speed of punch by getting off a couple of left hooks that hurt Tyson. In the second he stuck his head in but Tyson, in return, hit him low on the break. Then yet again Abell showed off Tyson's vulnerability by hitting him with sharp left counters that forced him to catch and hold.

Yet the crowd pleasing quality that comes through is the way Tyson loves to fight. Whenever Abell upped the pace and looked to attack, Tyson came back stronger and had him down twice in the third.

In the fourth Abell was still looking to attack although by now he was tiring and didn't have the punch to make Tyson back off. He was down twice as Tyson set him up with the jab then landed cracking right hands to the head. After the fourth knock down the referee stopped it and Abell didn't look too unhappy. Once again Tyson had shown what an all-round fighter he is. Even ring wise veterans like Abell don't know what's coming next and his confident invitation to opponents to come and make a fight of it isn't show boating, it's the way he feel. He never has a thought other than victory and wants to take the world on. After the fight he was telling Klitschko to come and have a go but trainer Peter Fury acknowledged he needed to lose another 14lbs and get into serious training.

"No One Beats Tyson Fury – At Talking!"

He said that himself and there's nothing Tyson likes better than getting the mike at a press conference and saying whatever comes into his head. He doesn't even need a mike, a TV camera will do and journalists come running because he usually says something worth reporting.

Tyson is proud of his Irish roots, proud to be a traveler, he calls himself a Gypsy Warrior. He believes that if the travelling community could be bothered to gain an education they'd be a force to be reckoned with because they're naturally smart, good at making money, striking deals. He says that by the time he was 18 he'd made £120,000 cash. by the time he was 18 he'd made £120,000 cash. Then lost it all at a casino. He's made plenty since and will make a lot more. Sometimes his tongue runs ahead of itself and he says things he will apologize for later. His remarks about homosexuality and abortion for example when he felt he was simply quoting the bible but it didn't come out that way.

Likewise his views on the place of women, they should be in the kitchen or on their back are thrown out for effect and a laugh. But there is a difference between what's thrown out by the ordinary person – and what the heavyweight champion of the world says to the press. In future he will probably appreciate that difference . . . on the other hand he may not.

When he's fighting he will be the centre of attraction, after the defeat of Klitschko he is the biggest thing in boxing and the sport needs an element of showbiz. Men who go into the ring and punch each other for a living are unlikely to be conventional types and he is a natural headline generator.

The legendary champion John L Sullivan was another one. Like Fury, he was the son of Irish and they share some colorful characteristics. They have the same spirit of the fighting Irish, a passion for fighting that makes them natural crowd pleasers. Both are controversial figures, collecting headlines along the way.

Sullivan was a pioneer. When he started his career boxing was illegal. He was the last bare knuckle champion but also the first to win the championship under the Marquis of Queensbury rules and wearing gloves. The Boston Strong Boy as he was known was so popular he has a claim to be the man who put boxing as a sport – and a business – on the map. He was boxing's first super star and loved the role. In the 1880s he beat all comers with his hammer like right hand yet he wasn't just a slugger. Sullivan was so athletic he was offered a chance to play professional baseball but he scented bigger money in the ring.

He was prepared to take on all comers and back himself to win. John L. toured from coast to coast Joe on what became known as the 'knocking out tour'. Louis had a 'bum of the month' run of fights, Sullivan's was more like 'bum of the night'.

In the ring his style has been compared to the best of Mike Tyson – and Floyd Patterson. A combination that would easily win him a title today!

Sullivan was a cheer leader at an important time for Irish Americans, just as the community was beginning to gain more influence and respect. The Irish were prominent in police forces, the construction business, politics and much else.

That presence continued through to President Kennedy, another son of a Boston Irish American family. On the boxing front the list of world champions included Irish American fighters like Gentleman Jim Corbett, Jack Dempsey, Gene Tunney and Billy Conn.

Tyson will be less keen to emulate a darker side of Sullivan. He was a notorious womanizer and drinker, an early hero for a tabloid press that was helping to promote boxing and, in spite of many scandals, turn it into a major sport.

There is every sign Tyson will continue to feature in press headlines, simply because he is an engaging character who says exactly what he thinks. More importantly he has a ring presence that will grow and grow.

His next fight was another meeting with Derek Chisora and the winner would be a mandatory challenger to Wladimir Klitschko. Since his first loss to Fury Chisora had been beaten by Vitali Klitschko, David Haye and Robert Helenius but bounced back with five wins. In press conferences Fury taunted Chisora, telling him every time he stepped up in class he got beaten. It was all part of selling the fight.

Fury came into the ring 10lbs lighter than his previous fight. He was serious but he also knew he had the beating of Chisora. From the first round he hit him with the jab any time he wanted. Chisora had said he wanted to fight like Joe Frazier, swarm all over Tyson but he didn't have the speed or the punch. Early on his corner was asking him, "Where's that beautiful hook?" He couldn't land it because Tyson was either keeping him away – or using his size to smother him. In some rounds Fury switched to southpaw and still the jab kept hitting the mark. In between rounds Chisora's corner was pleading with him to box and move, telling him he was better than this but he couldn't find an answer to Fury's power.

Steadily Tyson built up a lead and Chisora's face was getting beaten up, his right eye closed. He was too far behind on points and at the bell for the 10th his trainer told him it was "Now or never, no tears in the morning." Chisora tried a final attack but still Fury moved easily away, continued to stick out the jab and follow up with heavy rights. At the end of the round Chisora's corner pulled him out and nobody could argue. It was an emphatic win. Tyson had one more contest before he met Wladimir Klitschko. On paper it looked a dangerous fight against Christian Hammer, the German Heavyweight and WBO European champion but once again Tyson simply outclassed his opponent and at the end of the 10th round Hammer walked back to his corner shaking his head, he'd taken enough.

It was enough for the Gypsy Warrior too. He was ready to pack his bags, leave his modest hotel room in Bolton and jet off to claim the world title.

Eight British World Heavyweight Champions – Will Tyson Be The Greatest?

It's too early to say, as Chairman Mao said when he was asked if the French revolution had been a success. Mao probably had a view on boxing too. Something like – a long march to the hardest championship begins with a single punch.

Tyson can also afford to take the long view. He's won the title at 27, a time when he's not yet at his physical peak. Immediately after the Klitschko fight trainer Peter Fury said "Tonight you've only seen 65% of what Tyson can do." The Team is totally confident about a re-match but this is boxing, anything can happen.

Looking into the future and predicting he will retain the title for some time, how will he be rated alongside the other seven British world champions?

Starting at the beginning there's Cornishman Bob Fitzsimmons who won the title back in the 19th century. There were Fighting Furys around then too but boxing was very different. Fitzsimmons started off in bare knuckle days, he was a hard character with a tremendous punch and 59 KOs to prove it. But there's a tremendous size difference. Fitzsimmons was just under 6' and weighed around 12 stones. You'd have to say Tyson would beat him. His boxing skills, 14" advantage in reach and 6 stones in weight put him in a different league.

After Fitzsimmons there's a long gap to the next British champion, Lennox Lewis in 1992. Back in the 1930's Welsh boxer Tommy Farr came closer than anyone else when he gave Joe Louis a hard fight and Henry Cooper should have beaten Muhammad Ali after he put him down in their first fight. Cooper was cheated when Angelo Dundee slit Ali's glove in the interval to gain his man extra recovery time.

Lennox Lewis made the mistake of saying Tyson had absolutely no chance against Klitschko and looked very foolish when Tyson won convincingly. Since then the situation has gone from bad to worse in a Twitter storm. Lewis has a great career record and may feel he has never been given quite the recognition he deserved.

Tyson didn't improve his state of mind by saying he was "Old, jealous and a has been." In the ring it would be a very close fight, Lewis defeated every professional he ever faced and retired an undisputed champion. He owed a lot to Manny Steward who put more fluency, balance and a sharper jab into his boxing. Lewis defended his title successfully 14 times and had 32 KO's. He was too much for an ageing Mike Tyson but Vitali Klitschko gave him a hard time. He was fortunate to win, taking he decision after the referee stopped the fight following a cut to Klitschko.

Lewis had an outstanding and long career. He has a legitimate claim to be one of the greats, fighting better opponents than Tyson has faced so far. A true comparison is difficult but Tyson isn't at his peak yet. As he continues to develop he would probably stop Lewis. Definitely so if Lennox had an off night – he was susceptible to a one punch defeat. Tyson is certainly better for boxing, charisma wise it's no contest. A contemporary of Lewis said he was a good fighter but about as interesting as an instruction manual for toasters.

In the charisma stakes, another British former title holder, Frank Bruno, was well loved, respected and admired by British fans. But in the ring he didn't have the firepower to stop Tyson who would find Frank too often with his jab.

Three more British world title holders, Herbie Hide, Michael Bentt and Henry Akinwande would be overpowered by Tyson at his best. Akinwande fought and beat Tyson's father John which is another reason why he would lose.

Which leaves David Haye who always talked a brilliant fight . . . and then he met Wladimir Klitschko.

Haye went the distance but never really threatened an upset. He also predicted Tyson had "Only a one in twenty chance against Klitschko." He probably has a less than one in twenty chance of fighting Tyson now after he pulled out of a fight with him earlier. The new champion has said he would rather resign a belt than give him a payday. But of course money talks too – and often has the last word. So in time Haye may have his chance and get beaten up for good money.

Haye has begun a comeback after three years away from the ring and began with a 130 second, first round knockout of Australian journeyman Mark De Mori. In the ring afterwards Haye talked for longer than the fight lasted and tried to sound as if he had just beaten a rated fighter. He also said Tyson may only have got the decision in Germany against Klitschko because judges knew there was a rematch clause. Then he added, "Fury won't want to fight me, I punch too hard." It's just a shame he never off his punching power against Klitschko.

If Tyson keeps developing - as he has with every challenge so far - he will go down as the best British World Heavyweight champion of all time. He could even go further and move into the top ten heavyweight champions of all time.

Ali at his best would probably beat him, Larry Holmes, Sonny Liston, George Foreman and Joe Frazier too. But how about his father's great hero, Mike Tyson?

Taking the early Mike Tyson at his peak, and thinking about his mobility, then Fury would be in trouble. The side to side, up and down, constant movement of Tyson's style made him the most elusive of fighters and even Fury's extra reach would not help significantly. Neither would his size, Tyson couldn't be bullied. Iron Mike would probably concentrate on destructive body punches to slow Fury down then nail him with left hooks and right crosses. On the other hand . . . he may not.

Tyson Fury has immense self belief, mental strength and the talent to reach a higher level. Finally add in his natural advantages of size, reach and strength. Above all, he is a work in progress.

What Next For The New Champion?

One certainty is - he will be a big money earner. There are at least three fights that could propel him towards the Floyd Mayweather bracket of super stardom and riches. They are with Anthony Joshua, Deontay Wilder and a re-match with Wladimir Klitschko.

Joshua is a gold medal winner at the 2012 Olympics and has a professional record of 15 fights and 15 wins – all by KO. He is the current British, Commonwealth and WBC Heavyweight champion and ranked 9th in the heavyweight division by *Ring* magazine. His potential is huge. Joshua is 6' 6" tall and has a comparable reach to Tyson. He was born in Britain, spent time in Nigeria and has a mixed Nigerian/Irish background. Before taking up boxing he was a talented athlete with the rhythm and balance a top fighter needs. Although Joshua has not been around as long as Tyson he a crowd puller. Any fight between them will be a sell-out at the Wembley stadium and a global television hit.

But the big fight is with Deontay Wilder – the man who brought a heavyweight title back to the US for the first time in years. The WBC champion is unbeaten, he has the charisma, he has the clout and any contest with the Anglo Irish Tyson Fury a global smash hit.

Either of them would bring more world titles to Tyson and if he beat them both – he would be undisputed world champion. A position that's been vacant for some time.

Yet the next Fury fight is likely to be a rematch with Klitschko. The speculation is that Wladimir is smarting from his defeat and wants his titles back.

The difference is that in the negotiations Tyson will hold the whip hand and the Klitschkos won't enjoy that. There are also doubts about whether he really wants a re-match because he was well beaten.

When he was in his prime Sonny Liston was asked what was the biggest mistake his opponents made. "Getting in the ring with me," he replied with that frightening glare.

If Wladimir Klitschko is ever asked what his biggest mistake was he will probably think back to the night he got in the ring with Tyson Fury.

In the years to come he won't be the only one, Tyson is all set to become one of the truly big names in world boxing. A proud Gypsy Warrior with a reputation that can live alongside that of the great John L.

Printed in Great Britain
by Amazon